A CLEAN BILL OF WEALTH

THE 13 ESSENTIAL CATEGORIES OF FINANCIAL WELLNESS

A must-have guide to comprehensive wealth planning.

ANTHONY C. WILLIAMS
CWS, CHFC, RFC, CLU

A Clean Bill of Wealth

The 13 Essential Categories of Financial Wellness

Copyright © 2022 Anthony C. Williams

All rights reserved. No part of this book may be used or reproduced by any means, graphic, electronic, or mechanical, including photocopying, recording, taping or by any information storage retrieval system without the written permission of the publisher except in the case of brief quotations embodied in critical articles and reviews.

The information, ideas, and suggestions in this book are not intended to render professional advice. Before following any suggestions contained in this book, you should consult your personal accountant or other financial advisor. Neither the author nor the publisher shall be liable or responsible for any loss or damage allegedly arising as a consequence of your use or application of any information or suggestions in this book.

Legal Advice: The information, ideas, and suggestions in this book are not intended to render legal advice. Before following any suggestions contained in this book, you should consult your personal attorney. Neither the author nor the publisher shall be liable or responsible for any loss or damage allegedly arising as a consequence of your use or application of any information or suggestions in this book.

TABLE OF CONTENTS

INVESTMENT PLANNING & THE 3 PRIMARY INVESTMENT RISKS - 3

RISK MANAGEMENT & INSURANCE PLANNING - 8

BANKING & CREDIT MANAGEMENT - 13

RETIREMENT PLANNING - 17

EXECUTIVE COMPENSATION - 21

BUSINESS SUCCESSION PLANNING - 25

PLANNING FOR INCAPACITY - 29

TITLING & BENEFICIARY DESIGNATIONS - 34

EXECUTOR & TRUSTEE SELECTION - 39

EDUCATION & FAMILY SUPPORT - 44

CHARITABLE & PHILANTHROPIC GIVING - 47

DISTRIBUTION OF ESTATE - 52

TAX PLANNING - 58

FOREWORD
BY J. PHIL BUCHANAN, CWS®, CFP®

For more than a quarter of a century, Cannon Financial Institute has promoted and endorsed the "13 Wealth Management Issues" and the concept helped to lay the foundation for what is largely agreed upon to be "comprehensive wealth management" today. The novel idea then, was that advisors and their clients needed to look at the client's current financial situation today to determine where the client wanted to be at a fixed point in the future, then look at all of the various issues that can impede that plan. This was a shift towards helping families manage their wealth, and away from only managing the assets in a portfolio or trust. The financial services industry is as susceptible to disruption as every other industry. At the time, advisors used planning tools, like the typical "8.5" x 11" yellow note pad of paper to help understand the challenges their clients faced and to also explain how various solutions worked. We engaged in these activities in board rooms and kitchen tables in every community in the country. Technology disrupted how we worked, but the disruption brought benefits to the industry and our clients through the emergence of collaborative financial planning tools that complement innovative digital banking experiences. Competition disrupted our industry as well, with some of the larger investment firms seemingly engaged in a race that brought us to incredibly low or no fees for certain investment management services. Again, the industry and clients benefited through the creation of innovative solutions and higher levels of services for which clients were willing to pay.

The year 2020 saw more change and disruption for Americans in one year than many have seen in half of their lifetimes. Due to the novel virus and a lack of clarity regarding liability and potential responsibility, the COVID-19 pandemic saw not only the cancelation of high-profile events but confinement for many senior citizens within nursing homes and extended care facilities. Many individuals went into the hospital experiencing respiratory issues never coming back home to see their family and loved ones. How many of us went to the doctor for an appointment and thought to ensure that our assets were titled properly, that our wills and trusts were updated, and that all of our financial accounts had the right beneficiary designations? Not many. Many never came home to get those affairs in order.

As the country dealt with the initial and long-term fallout of the pandemic, disruption happened again. Financial planning was already important, but the idea of talking about the issues that didn't generate fees for the advisor or institution was relatively new.

It was not top-of-mind to talk about things like "Planning for

Incapacity" nor to conduct "Titling & Beneficiary Designation Reviews" because there were no new financial instruments to use or additional monies exchanging hands. Putting the "13 Wealth Management Issues" front and center and helping to make the less-exciting Wealth Issues take a more important role has been some of the most rewarding work that Cannon Financial has contributed to our clients and our client's clients. Many of you reading this likely work in the medical field, so you are used to many of the procedural changes that happened very quickly in the field of healthcare. However, in finance, while some rules have changed around taxes and retirement; the core principles are still there. It's important to have a financial plan in place, all documents updated with your clearest intentions articulated therein. If you own your practice, it's even more important that you have your personal finances and key decisions in order, but also plans that allow your business to continue to function or transfer seamlessly.

No one really could have predicted the impacts of COVID-19 or the fact that so many were not able to get their financial plans in place and intentions documented. We always think there will be time.

When Anthony talked about the idea of this book, no one knew what would happen as a result of COVID. We've all been impacted and now know that it can happen again.

What lessons have you learned over the last few years? How has it impacted how you make plans and provisions? If you have not talked to your advisor about ensuring you have a documented financial plan and set of clear intentions, why not?

The 13 Wealth Management Issues, outlined in Anthony's and my colleague Chris' work, definitely reflect upon each issue's relevance in our current time. But we don't know what's next and what the next challenges might be. We can only control what we can control. Ensuring that your plan and your intentions are documented and that you have had an intentional discussion with your financial advisory team about each of the 13 Wealth Management Issues described within this book is likely a very good first step.

J. Phil Buchanan, CWS®, CFP®
Executive Chairman
Cannon Financial Institute

The content of this book is for informational or educational purposes only and does not take into account the investment objectives or financial situation of any client or prospective clients. The information is not intended as investment advice and is not a recommendation about managing or investing your retirement savings. Clients seeking information regarding their particular investment needs should contact a financial professional.

INTRODUCTION

Over the years it's pretty common to hear the question, "What does comprehensive or holistic mean?" with respect to financial planning. It's a solid question. Many people call themselves financial advisors when in reality, they are simply salespeople. There is nothing wrong with being a salesperson. We buy cars and mattresses from well-qualified salespeople. However, we do not entrust our retirement plans and our most important financial decisions, often with significant tax consequences, to salespeople. For a financial salesperson, the scope of their practice is often limited to one particular aspect of financial planning they can directly service or sell, e.g., investments, stocks/bonds, or insurance/risk management.

As comprehensive Wealth Advisors, it's our belief that having separate conversations about subjects simply isn't effective from a planning perspective. Rather, it's critical to integrate all the key wealth management issues into one holistic dialogue addressing every clients' unique goals and objectives without regard for our ability to "sell" you something. Helping our clients' spot financial issues that may negatively impact them and then helping them understand *how* these issues will ultimately impact other interrelated personal and financial goals is the cornerstone of our advisory practice.

This being the case, let's introduce those **13 Wealth Management Issues** which most consistently impact our clients and their families:

1) Investment Planning
2) Risk Management & Insurance Planning
3) Banking & Credit Management
4) Retirement Planning
5) Executive Compensation
6) Business Succession Planning
7) Planning for Incapacity
8) Titling & Beneficiary Designations
9) Executor & Trustee Selection
10) Education & Family Support
11) Charitable & Philanthropic Giving
12) Distribution of Estate
13) Tax Planning

When considering these issues, it's important to ask yourself, how do any of these affect you, your family, and your goals?

The following chapters will cover each of these **Wealth Management Issues** in greater detail. Our hope is this book will provide educational but also promote thought, leading to action...in a holistic manner, of course.

INVESTMENT PLANNING & THE 3 PRIMARY INVESTMENT RISKS
ISSUE NUMBER 1 OUT OF 13

At first glance, the phrase **Investment Planning** likely seems fairly straightforward. We have money. We invest. We hope for positive outcomes. Although a typically held view of investment planning, our position is this subject has much greater depth; particularly a number of common risks to which investors expose themselves unnecessarily. A comprehensive view of Investment Planning begins with gathering a full inventory of ALL assets..................**ALL** assets. Too often, clients and advisors alike, take a segmented approach. Let's review the 401k. Let's review the IRA. Let's review the 529. Let's review the brokerage account. Etc. Etc. Etc. **Holistic Wealth Planning** evaluates all assets comprehensively in an effort to make sure certain risks aren't being taken on. Really, this approach is a philosophic approach. Our investment philosophy is rooted in the feelings our clients have with respect to risk. After conducting a disciplined discovery process and an individualized risk profile questionnaire to determine what type of investments are appropriate, we utilize a three-tiered approach whereby various investment strategies are aligned with clients' goals.

Often, **AFTER** gathering a client's full inventory of investments and having an in-depth conversation about their goals/expectations and risk profile--and **PRIOR** to discussing actual strategy--our process includes reviewing **Three Primary Investment Risks:**

1) **Inappropriate Asset Allocation**
2) **Failure to Monitor and Maintain Asset Allocation**
3) **Lack of Correlation**

Inappropriate Asset Allocation

A thorough review of a client's situation, future, feelings, family dynamics, complexity, goals, risk tolerance, and time horizon is critical. The benefit of an advisor is objectivity...being detached *emotionally*. Often, we review portfolios with significant overlap in asset allocation due to a segmented approach to individual accounts rather than a comprehensive view. *Note: having multiple advisors virtually ensures your asset allocation will be inappropriate.*

Failure to Monitor and Maintain Asset Allocation

Your portfolio is not static. Market forces are often like Mother Nature. All over the place! This being the case, it's critical to have a disciplined and systematic process for review and rebalancing. Additionally, your life, which isn't static either, may dictate changes to your portfolio and risk. *Note: having multiple advisors significantly increases this risk.* Regularly monitoring your portfolio and your feelings about risk on a regular basis are strongly advised.

Lack of Coordination

Each investment must interrelate appropriately without overlaps or gaps to ensure success. **Lack of Coordination** leads to overlap which simply means your portfolio is not balanced appropriately. **Concentration Risk** is when a client has too much exposure to one stock or one sector. Additionally, this risk often leads to the risk of missed opportunities when other sectors do well.

To offset this final risk, our approach is to take a three-tiered approach utilizing **Traditionally Asset Allocated Investments**, **Opportunistic Investments**, and **Guarded Investments**. Traditional investments include equities, fixed income, and cash. Stocks. Bonds. Exchange-traded funds. The strategies you google. Where we differentiate and where we assess appropriate asset correlation is via Opportunistic Investments. These strategies include asset classes which do NOT correlate with the market. In some respects, these options provide a hedge against traditional market risk. Utilizing publicly non-traded real estate investment trusts, oil/gas, 1031 exchange, Business Development Companies, leasing programs, etc., for a portion of a portfolio may enhance diversification. Finally, Guarded Investments. Certain types of investments protect you against market decreases, i.e., no risk of market loss, grow and distribute tax-free, while also providing layers of asset protection against lawsuits and creditors. Implementing our three-tiered approach goes beyond the traditional modality of asset allocation providing clients with a unique platform to pursue their goals and objectives.

Consider this medically-based example: If you need to have your knee reconstructed, would you have a different Orthopaedist work on your MCL, another work on your PCL, and yet another on your ACL? Of course not. What risks would that pose to the patient? What would happen if there was zero coordination amongst those surgeons?

Moreover, could you ever trust any of those surgeons again for exposing you to those risks without properly explaining them to you so you could make a different decision? Would you let them operate independently? You'd probably say, "I'd never do that in 100 years!" But if you did, what would you have to do to make sure the procedure had a favorable outcome? You would probably have to have a meeting with all three Orthopaedists to discuss specifically what each of them would be doing while also making sure their respective teams are working collaboratively. Now... consider your current investment and retirement goals. If you have assets with more than one advisory firm, who is responsible for coordinating the 'operation' among your investment advisors/Orthopaedic surgeons? Who is responsible on your team for creating that alignment? In the investment world, we call those choices asset allocation. **Asset allocation** is the choices and strategies that your advisors put together to help you pursue your goals while mitigating as much risk as possible. In the same way you should trust your surgeon to explain all possible risks to which you are exposed, you should expect this from your advisor or wealth strategy team. If you have money currently invested with 2-4 advisory firms, who is on point to coordinate between them and mitigate those risks?

If it's your responsibility to be coordinating your team, you might need some help with that coordination. But there are other risks. In addition to managing that risk of lack of coordination of asset allocation, there is the issue of alignment within each of those portfolios. Then there is the ongoing assessment to make sure the portfolios are working together as market conditions change or more likely, your life goals and circumstances change. The surgical analogy only works so far because that's a single event; not a lifetime of saving for your retirement.

In summary, our disciplined process provides insights into your current situation, your future goals, your feelings with respect to the market, a review of risk, and ultimately an analysis with our findings. On an ongoing basis, our wealth management platform, Mosaic Wealth Portal, provides each individual goal the ability to determine if you are on track to meet each objective in real-time. Our continued philosophy of goals-based reporting is never more prevalent. There is nothing more important to a client than having the confidence their goals are on track and being pursued effectively.

Investments in securities do not offer a fix rate of return. Principal, yield and/or share price will fluctuate with changes in market conditions and, when sold or redeemed, you may receive more or less than originally invested. No system or financial planning strategy can guarantee future results. Therefore, no current or prospective client should assume that future performance or any specific investment, investment strategy or product will be profitable.

RISK MANAGEMENT & INSURANCE PLANNING
ISSUE NUMBER 2 OUT OF 13

Hopefully, you found the investment planning entry of benefit. Now, let's move from investment planning to a discussion of risk and insurance planning. From a practical perspective, what is **Risk Management & Insurance Planning**? It's protecting you, your family, and your wealth. There are myriad strategies, layers if you will, to protecting your wealth. In broad strokes, insurance is the vehicle(s) discussed in this chapter. However, which type of insurance? For what purpose? Pros? Cons? These are all important considerations.

Most of our clients initially consider insurance as a tool for protecting their goals, their business, and their family. But insurance can be used independently or paired with other financial instruments to pursue and protect goals. Insurance is a unique financial tool.

Consider that there are no other financial instruments that can offer protection along with a savings option, an investment option, long-term care options, and the list goes on. There are **four** primary types of insurance: **life**, **disability**, **long-term care**, and **liability**. In addition to allowing protection of assets from loss or damage, it can also be used to solve both personal and business financial problems. Here are the questions you should be asking yourself: Most of our clients have some form of insurance. As there are several types and uses, along with limitations, a common refrain when asked to review existing policies is, "I already have insurance." The short answer is, "Good. Very smart." The long answer is, "Good. How often do you review those policies and make adjustments when your personal and financial situation changes?"

You might ask yourself, "Why is a wealth strategist writing about insurance?" We help people pursue and protect their financial and personal goals. Our commitment to our clients is to help them reach those goals. Consider when you purchased the policies you currently have. Has your family situation changed? Do you have more children or grandchildren now? Have you changed jobs or started a business or new practice? Think about your current policies and then consider:

1) Do I have the right amount?
2) Is it structured properly?
3) Is the cost appropriate?

How do these questions relate to the most common types of insurance?

Life Insurance

Life insurance alone can be used for liquidity for taxes, funds to transfer a business, replacement of charitable gift/philanthropic objectives, reduction of debt, and equalization of inheritances. All types of insurance should be assessed from **three** vantage points:

adequacy of coverage, **appropriateness of policies**, and **cost-effectiveness**. We often conduct an efficiency analysis with our clients to address the questions above. Recently, we had a conversation with a client and asked when they last conducted an efficiency analysis on their life insurance. The reply: "What's an efficiency analysis?" The answer went something like this: "Have you known anyone who refinanced their mortgage in the past few years? Why did they take this action?"

Likely the answer is lower payments, costs, or interest rate. Wouldn't it make sense to take the same approach on your life insurance? Our goal for our clients is to make sure their insurance structures are as efficient as possible. If you are a business owner or head of a professional practice, life insurance can be used to both retain and incentivize key employees, as well as protect your business.

Disability Insurance

Disability insurance is fairly straightforward. If you are a specialist/professional, have an acute issue, and are unable to work (income-producing duties of your specialty) it's CRITICAL to have income protection insurance or said another way, wealth preservation insurance. The financial loss to you without disability insurance is likely catastrophic. For example, say you earn $500k and are 40 years old. What if you were disabled for 25 years? Your financial loss is $12.5MM. My guess is for most reading this chapter, it's more than their car and home...combined...times four. Yet, people routinely do not hesitate to acquire car and homeowners insurance. It's not close.

Long-Term Care Insurance

Long-term care is interesting for higher net worth folks. Often, the statement made is, "I'm going to self-insure that!" As a result, if, or rather **WHEN** incapacity hits, the costs are paid out of cash flow and accumulated net worth. Our approach is to take the following steps: **Identify Potential Risk**, **Evaluate Existing Resources**, **Determine Potential Gaps (exposures)**, and **Consider Strategic Options**. The questions we typically ask are, "What formal arrangements have you made to plan for incapacity?", or "If without warning you couldn't take care of yourself, what would be your ideal situation?", or "Walk me through what would happen if something were to happen to you..." After addressing these questions and following a disciplined approach, one of two outcomes becomes clear: **1) Self-insuring will work** or **2) Self-insuring will NOT work**. How quickly would you want to know?

Liability Insurance

Liability insurance on a personal level is handled via your Property & Casualty agents, like State Farm or American Family. Our role as an advisor is to queue you to when increasing coverage is sensible. Think of this as your personal malpractice insurance. You are already familiar with the costs of insurance from your malpractice insurance and your liability insurance. Those are in fact helping you protect your business and your family. Fewer people consider that you can use insurance to *pursue* goals as well as using insurance to *protect* their goals. As you are able to discern, again, there are a lot of moving parts. The key is to take a disciplined approach of discovery and make certain to address the three questions noted above for each type of insurance in concert with one another.

The cost and availability of life insurance depends on factors such as age, health, and type and amount of insurance purchased. Before implementing a strategy involving life insurance, it would be prudent to make sure that you are insurable by having the policy approved. As with most financial decisions, there are expenses associated with the purchase of life insurance. Policies commonly have mortality and expense charges. In addition, if a policy is surrendered prematurely, there may be surrender charges and income tax implications.

BANKING & CREDIT MANAGEMENT
ISSUE NUMBER 3 OUT OF 13

Typical conversations heard between advisors and their clients most often revolve around ways the client can benefit from specific investment strategies and services offered by the investment firm. While cashflow of your business or cash positions might be a passing conversation, including, using debt or leverage appropriately; there are not many times where banking and or credit management would likely be a topic that investment managers want to explore. Why?

These are often financial strategies they cannot participate in due to fee structures that are tied to the management of the assets. Short and long-term goals require capital and many business goals within your practice may revolve around borrowing in order to hit those goals. If your "holistic" advisor doesn't discuss financial goals outside of investments and insurance, are they really being holistic?

Are they really working in your best interest? Firms like ours, which take a truly objective, financial planning-based approach, could not make well-informed recommendations regarding your financial wellness if they didn't understand the full financial picture, recognize your personal and professional goals, and learn about your feelings and thoughts on debt and leverage. To clarify the difference, *debt* is utilized for large purchases you might not otherwise be able to afford. *Leverage* should be considered an instrument whereby the margin is geared towards increasing return on investment...typically on a longer-term basis. Often, the primary drivers of usage integrate **financial sensibility and emotional sensitivity**; namely, feelings about debt.

There are **five key questions** to consider:

1) **What are your family and your practice's short and long-term goals?** The goal here is to understand how you plan to fund each goal. Cash? Debt? Realized gains from securities and investments?

2) **What are the cashflow needs of your family and your practice?** How can debt be used to mitigate a cash crunch? Do we have access to particular cash sources to cover a short-term cash issue?

3) **In addition to personal and professional goals, are there financial goals that require investment of capital to create wealth?** Is there a clear understanding of how liabilities can leverage wealth? It's important to have a clear understanding of your perspective with respect to debt and how specific strategies may provide benefits.

4) **How are liabilities/leverage coordinated with your wealth plan?** The coordination of these components MIGHT enhance returns if structured properly.

5) **Are you familiar with the relationship between tax efficiency and utilization of debt? What are your thoughts and feelings about taxes?** There are several potential options to evaluate: Residence, HELOC, Investments, and properly structured cash value life insurance. It's no secret that interest rates are at historic lows. Firms and advisors that truly take a financial planning-based approach need to understand your goals, both personal and professional. There are only **three** primary economic engines: **investments, insurance,** and **cash.** True holistic advisors cannot ignore cashflow and credit. You should expect your advisor to discuss every aspect of your financial wellness in order for them to provide advice and guidance that is in your personal or professional best interest.

So, you might be thinking, what are the steps involved to determine if debt/leverage is appropriate for me. Ask yourself the following questions. First, how do you view debt? Is it a tool or something you must eliminate? What is your comfort level? Second, do you have in place a written cash flow summary which ensures coordination of liabilities/leverage and your wealth? Third, is the strategy appropriately structured such that you're maximizing the leverage while incorporating maximum tax efficiencies? Finally, in the event of a short-term cash crunch, would it be preferred to have a line of credit or some form of cash available (so long as it doesn't create disharmony)?

The bottom line is to understand your goals that will require short or long-term capital, determine your perspective on debt, and then have a comprehensive conversation to evaluate if particular strategies may provide you, your family and/or your business new opportunities.

RETIREMENT PLANNING
ISSUE NUMBER 4 OUT OF 13

It is often said that there are only three primary engines to power the achievement of any final goal. In the previous chapters, we covered these primary drivers of financial goal achievement: **Investment Planning**, **Risk Management & Insurance Planning**, and **Banking and Credit Management**. This chapter, Retirement Planning, certainly involves a number of variables, but retirement planning leverages all three of the previous identified Wealth Management Issues.

Let's face it, for many of us Retirement Planning IS Financial Planning. They are one-in-the-same. This is the number one issue on the minds of our clients.

When considering Retirement Planning, we find our clients to be in one of four distinct phases on the retirement journey. You are either in the **Accumulation**, **Transition**, **Utilization**, or **Transfer** phase.

These stages are generally defined by age and health of our clients. Those clients who are early and mid-career are in the

Accumulation phase. This is primarily the savings phase, and it lasts until around age 55. From age 55-65, we begin to make full preparations for your retirement and help you gather various savings plans you've started along the way and help you sift through important Social Security decisions. On the other side of this triangle, are the **Utilization** and **Transfer** phases. Here we help clients adapt to living within their planned budget while living their fullest life that they have earned and for which they have planned. Finally, we help ensure that family and future generations receive any remaining retirement benefits available, plus help establish a legacy should that be their intention.

No two retirement plans are alike. Like people, retirement plans are individual and deeply personal. Regardless of the stage in which you may find yourself, there are **four** common risk factors that often weigh on the minds of our clients.

Risk Factors of Retirement

These risks pertain to **Longevity**, **Inflation**, **Long-term Incapacity**, and **Sequence of Returns**. In addition to the risk factors, here are the **common questions** that we hear our clients ask every day and help them address.

1) **Longevity:** How long should you plan to save? How long will you live? Will you outlive your money? How much will retirement cost?

2) **Inflation:** How will the inflation rate to change when you retire? What can we expect? How will this affect your nest egg?

3) **Long-Term Incapacity:** Are we prepared for an unexpected illness? Healthcare costs? Live at home? What type of assistance is preferred & affordable? If you require long-term care, what costs should your family expect?

4) **Sequence of Returns:** What is the withdrawal rate? When should you begin to draw upon Social Security? Is waiting best for you to reap the higher payout from Social Security? What tools are being used to assess likelihood of success? What happens if you do not need to use some of your retirement money, but the law dictates you need to take distributions?

Have you adequately considered these risks and how these may impact your retirement planning? Often, we've noticed that people will spend more time planning a trip next year than they will planning out a twenty or thirty-year retirement. It certainly is more fun to think about that vacation. However, after spending some time discussing your vision for retirement, you will find you will be more relaxed when pondering that next vacation because your retirement plan is in good hands.

With life expectancies increasing and some individuals wanting to retire early, the need for a sound retirement plan is crucial. We must examine the results of using distributions from the plan during life versus distributing to descendants at death. There are many issues to consider including **timing of distributions, taxation - income & estate**, as well as the **degree of control** preferred. The risks and concerns we've presented are the most common. Perhaps you have additional concerns, and we can help ease your mind. You've worked hard to save, so let's plan to help you make the most of your retirement.

Hopefully in this brief chapter, you are able to discern how important implementing a disciplined process with collaboration with CPAs and attorneys will be to you and your retirement.

EXECUTIVE COMPENSATION
ISSUE NUMBER 5 OUT OF 13

This next Wealth Management Issue, Executive Compensation, definitely has a targeted audience but it can be a bit misleading. There are some specific details which might impact you if you are one of the "top four" employees in your company. However, many of these issues impact highly compensated employees making more than $120,000 per year, not just the most senior executives of a firm. In this chapter, we will also review a three-pronged discussion from more of a big picture perspective. When evaluating these issues, it is no surprise that primary considerations include strategies to **maximize worth** and **minimize taxation** both currently and from an estate planning or transfer perspective. Let's do this.

The first issue to address is the broadly overused term "executive" as it regards to complex compensation issues. Unless you are retired, if you are employed you are likely receiving some form of compensation. The higher you climb in your company or your practice, the more complex your compensation plan will be. Why? Because we know that firms use tools like benefit plans, deferred compensation, insurance contracts, and equity as a way of incentivizing you to remain at their firm. Gone are the days when only "executives" earn incentive stock plans and equity. This is a common compensation tool for tech start-ups and other practice groups that may be cash-strapped in early days of the business. Many employees earned bonuses and often we don't consider that our salary, benefits, short-term incentives like annual or performance bonuses, and longer-term equity compensation are all taxed at different levels. Your salary is taxed at the normal income tax rates. Taxes on benefits are all determined by which qualified plans or non-qualified plans in which you participate. Tax law changes last year means that many perks are now taxes. Bonuses are often taxed at different rates from ordinary income. Long term incentives often paid via equity compensation will be different based on when and how you exercise your shares.

So even if you are not an "executive" in your firm, but you have multiple retirement plans and equity compensation, you likely need to speak with a professional for guidance and advice. Let's look at some other common issues pertaining to compensation.

Commonly, we see executives and other highly compensated employees concerned with the impact of taxation on their various stock options plans, deferred compensation, qualified & non-qualified plans. Why? Because this and ultimately impacts their net worth & how their goals will be affected. There are a number of compensation options including: Cash, Deferred Compensation, Life Insurance, Qualified Plans, Non-qualified Plans, Incentive Stock

Options (ISO), and Non-qualified Stock Options (NQSO). The decisions you have to make about the types of equity compensation you have when you exercise your options can ultimately cost you thousands of dollars in taxes if you do not act with precise timing. Here are some examples of the most typical client interactions we have involving these options. Often, we engage in a three-pronged discussion of compensation:

1) **Compensatory Review:** Compare with current ISO, NQSO, restricted stock, employee stock purchase plans, and stock appreciation rights plans. Goals include maximizing tax efficiency and control.

2) **Insurance:** Non-Qualified/Supplemental, Long-term Care, Health, Life, & Disability Insurance. In all cases, we are evaluating adequacy, appropriateness and cost effectiveness.

3) **Qualified & Non-Qualified:** Evaluate the alternatives and develop a strategy for distribution.

When combining the three of these aspects of compensation, the long-term strategy generally becomes developing a lifetime income plan AND efficient wealth transfer.

It's important that clients understand a number of factors, including whether stock options are qualified or non-qualified; restrictions associated with the timing of exercising or selling options, tax implications, and decisions on how the exercise is funded. Our goal is to make sure that you retain as much of your hard-earned compensation as possible, and a common mistake is that executives and highly compensated employees don't pause to discuss their compensation with their financial advisor. If your overreaching goal is tax minimization, efficient wealth accumulation, lifetime income needs, and transferring your wealth to your family or causes of your choice, then we are here to talk about all aspects of your financial life, including providing guidance about aspects of your compensation. Our commitment to you is to deliver a plan that provides you with the greatest chance to realize your family's or practice's goals while being highly considerate of your current situation, your outlook on the future, your feelings, and your family dynamics.

Your financial advisors should be aware of all of these moving parts as they are gears and cogs in your greatest recurring asset, your compensation. Ultimately, it's important your advisors are working collaboratively explaining the nuance of your compensation, the subsequent investment strategy, taxation and how these items impact your financial planning objectives.

BUSINESS SUCCESSION PLANNING
ISSUE NUMBER 6 OUT OF 13

The sixth wealth management issue in our series centers around a topic with a slightly misleading title, **Business Succession Planning**. Like the other wealth issue, it's critical to have an in-depth discussion regarding the owners' goals & objectives. Before you could even think about transferring your business to a partner or family, your advisor needs to ensure that both your personal and business needs are being addressed during the tenure of your ownership.

We know that before you can get to the finish line and transfer your practice, there are several other issues you will face along the way, just like you face them with your personal wealth.

So far, we have written about several topics about which you should expect to communicate with your advisor. In addition to your investments and asset allocation; you should be having conversations about your retirement, your family's risk management and insurance plans, your cash flow and debt strategies, your education and eldercare planning needs, your charitable inclinations, etc. But what about your business? We know that your practice is likely your primary source of your wealth and thus, if your business needs are not handled, there is little chance that your personal wealth will grow. What role should your advisor have in your business?

Your trusted advisor should be talking about your personal financial goals, as well as your business goals. Your advisor should discuss issues that can help you grow your practice, not just items that grow the practice of your advisor. These should be discussions around your working capital and how you are managing cash flow/liquidity. Will you need to make investments in more equipment? Will you plan to open a second or third location and require additional real estate? If so, are you discussing how you will fund or leverage that expansion.

You've likely talked about your personal retirement, but what about the retirement plans of those in your employment in your practice? You have covered your personal risk management strategy, but what about the protection needs of your business?

Your financial advisor should be advising you on your *entire* financial life, not just your personal wealth. This will eventually bring us to the transfer of your business. It should, like so many things that have made you successful, be **intentional**. It should be very intentional.

Transferring the ownership of a business is time consuming, complex, and often emotional for the party that is exiting the business. There are **four options** for a business owner:

1) **To transfer to children/descendants during life.**

2) To transfer to children/descendants before death.

3) To sell the business to employees or a third-party entity during life.

4) To sell the business to employees or a third-party entity before death.

Each of these options are available to business owners during their lives or after their deaths. Planning for this inevitable transfer is the key. The timing of the transfer or sale, and the resulting transfer tax or income tax issues, need to be addressed in each business owner's wealth management plan. Additionally, and likely expectedly, the nature and type of taxation and planning requires specific focus as transfer taxes will be determined not by Congress and the IRS, but by your ability to plan for this event. Annual exclusion/exemption. Lifetime gift exemption. Transfer interests. Estate tax considerations. Capital gain considerations. Asset protection. Transfer strategies. These are conversations you should be having with your wealth strategist and/or advisor.

When we begin discussions with our business owner clients, we find they fall into **one of three categories:**

1) **Fully Funded Plan:** Plan contains clear instructions and documentation for successors and heirs.

2) **Unfunded Succession Plan:** Plans are drawn up but lack funding of buy-sell agreements, for example.

3) **Undocumented Succession Plan:** There is a lack of any plan or documentation about the intentions.

The biggest risk a business owner maintains is the failure of having a written and/or unfunded exit plan or everything would need to go without a hitch to achieve the stated goals. In many cases, folks are "too busy" or it doesn't seem urgent. In other cases, clients are overwhelmed. Often our commentary to clients is something to the effect of "Why work for a lifetime to build something so special and meaningful to you/your family and then leave it in jeopardy?!" Important considerations or conversations to have include:

1) If something happened to you, what happens to the company?
2) Do you have a formal written plan?
3) Is your plan funded?
4) Do your successors KNOW what the plan is?

There are many moving parts to managing and growing your business; succession planning is just *one of many* critical components. If your current advisor isn't talking to you about your working capital needs or funding future expansion, are you really getting the best advice and counsel? It's critical to integrate the tangible logistical components with the emotional and family-based considerations. Be sure to discuss your business goals with your advisor, not just your personal financial details. When it finally comes to transition and succession planning, the bottom line is to develop a plan based on all the information above and move forward judiciously.

PLANNING FOR INCAPACITY
ISSUE NUMBER 7 OUT OF 13
SPECIAL PROTECTION STRATEGIES EDITION PART 1 OUT OF 3

This is the first of a special three-part chapter series on basic protection strategies that every reader (and their family) should take very seriously following the beginning of the COVID-19 era. Many of the other chapters concern your goals, your investments, your insurance coverage, or retirement. In these next three chapters, we are going to focus on preparing for the unexpected. In part one, we will address on common concern that has impacted thousands and thousands of families: **Incapacity**.

You'd be hard pressed to have imagined what we have gone through and experienced with regards to the novel COVID-19 virus during the first few months of 2019. This was not on the radar of the average citizen at the beginning of the year, let-alone last year when many readers likely last had their annual reviews with their advisors.

Now that we are coming to terms with the aftermath of the COVID-19 outbreak and businesses are forced to start operating differently and people are interacting differently, it is the right time to think about something else differently; **financial planning**. What can we learn? What should we do differently?

Prior to the COVID-19 virus, the common response to suggestions regarding discussion about the planning of one's personal incapacity sounded something like this: "Whoever wants to talk about this?" As the virus spread, it became "The odds of catching that are so small!" and "It won't happen to us." The sheer number of people impacted by the virus should cause us all to take a brief pause. Too often, we all read or hear stories about people being admitted to the hospital and then remaining in isolation for the remainder of their life. For these individuals, it is not yet clear how many had their basic affairs in order. They saw no one ever again.

But imagine if you were taken seriously ill today, as you read this, and were never allowed to see your spouse, your children, your business partner? What if you never were able to see anyone again?

The question to now consider is simple. If that was you, do you have everything in order in your personal financial life and with your business? If you never had the opportunity to speak to a business partner or your employees, would your practice survive long-enough to be sold? Did you have documents like power-of-attorney in place so that trusted family members or your business partner could make decisions based upon your best interests and intentions? You may have a plan, but is it written down, signed, and witnessed?

You don't even need to be caught up by all of the media sensation and political sensation to take a few moments and make sure that your trusted family members and business partners have legal authority to make decisions on your behalf in the event that you can no longer make them yourself. There are reasons to do this well-beyond anything related to COVID-19.

As people age, the reality of their situation becomes more apparent. At some point, something might happen to us that may incapacitate us. However, it is still a conversation that most people, regardless of the facts, do not want or care to have. All of that being true, **planning for incapacity** is a crucial component of any wealth management or financial plan. When thinking about having confidence that your wishes will be followed, once again, planning in advance rears its head. Our experience suggests (as does the data) that most people would prefer to choose someone to act on their behalf, rather than have that person appointed for them by a court.

Since this is a significant decision, it's important to bring up **three concerns** with regard to a clients' durable **Power of Attorney:**

1) **Who is named?**
2) **Is this person knowledgeable of where the pertinent documents are located?**
3) **Who does the incapacitated person have confidence to be consulted by the Attorney-in-Fact?**

When considering planning for incapacity the **common mistakes** include:

1) **Failure to draft a plan.** Planning with advisors is key.
2) **Failure to designate responsible/legal parties.** Assess the nature of your relationships.
3) **Not naming primary & secondary parties.** These include

Power of Attorney, Successor, Trustee.

4) **Failure to disclose the document/plan.** Notification of and location of documents is key.

5) **Failure in communicating expectations, as well as the role of advisors.**

These same issues apply to business owners as well, except the impacts might be greater as employees, suppliers, and clients could be impacted as well.

Naturally, there are other issues to consider when thinking about **Incapacity Planning**. Hopefully, this is a starting point for you to begin the process to protect your family and your family's wealth. It is important to make sure that you have a plan, you have shared your intentions with family members and partners, and that you have a written this plan down and stored it in a safe location should the time come to use it. A suitable place to start is sitting down with your advisor and drafting a plan for who will make financial and life decisions for you in the event you cannot. Tens of thousands of people found themselves in the situation of not ever being able to speak to their trusted family members and business partners again. It is hard to blame them when they really did not think anything like this was possible.

That was before. This is now. And now is different. Now we can learn from the experiences of others. Set up some time to talk with your advisor so that you can solidify your plan to make sure that your financial intentions and interests are protected and that decisions can be made that are in line with the way you intend.

A CLEAN BILL OF WEALTH

For a comprehensive review of your personal situation, always consult with a tax or legal advisor. Neither Cetera Advisors LLC nor any of its representatives may give legal or tax advice.

TITLING & BENEFICIARY DESIGNATIONS
ISSUE NUMBER 8 OUT OF 13
SPECIAL PROTECTION STRATEGIES EDITION PART 2 OUT OF 3

This is part two in our three-part special chapter series on **Protection Strategies**.

In part one of this series in the era of COVID-19, we looked at steps you can take to make plans in the event of your incapacity or plans you can make to mitigate the financial complications of incapacity of a loved one. This particular Wealth Management Issue, **Titling & Beneficiary Designations**, seems as if it should be fairly straightforward, but it is not. In a perfect world, the titling of your assets/wealth are congruent with your beneficiary designations, wills, and preferences. After all, when you open an account or take out a policy, you are completing those sections with valid information at that given time. But times change. Spouses change. The number of dependents change. We have the best intentions to change all of those accounts and paperwork as our life changes, but life often gets in the way. We think we will have time to complete those tasks until it's too late.

The initial question you might have is "I get that this is an important Protection Strategy, but what does this have to do with COVID-19?". Good question. The answer is simply that we do not know when life can change, or when circumstances can change, and we no longer have time to change what we intended to change.

You likely know about how a **will** works, but assets transfer in a couple of ways within our society. One way is through ensuring that an asset can transfer to a beneficiary that is in accordance with their wishes. If the assets themselves are titled with joint ownership or if there is a beneficiary, it is the easiest way for the asset to transfer posthumously. If the assets do not have beneficiaries designated, then the assets pass to the power of the executor/executrix and can be used to pay for the expenses of the estate unless there is other guidance within the will. The most direct way to transfer an asset is to either title it in a way that it is jointly owned or to use the beneficiary designation to ensure the asset transfers upon death. But what does this have to do with COVID-19?

Simple. During the peak of the 2020 pandemic, many hospitals were at max capacity and nursing homes were on lockdown. This meant that if a family member or loved one was being treated in the hospital or residing in a nursing home, the facilities were locked down and family members and executors had no access to make legal changes based on a sick person's final wishes and intentions. Many people entered hospitals and never saw their family members again due to the isolation efforts. Even if they were able to speak or if they were cogent and able to make their own sound decisions, they never had the opportunity to speak to their families or their advisors to make those changes.

Consider even the most basic risks associated with this wealth issue. For example, say you are a divorced person with a life insurance policy where the ex-spouse is the still the beneficiary of the policy. In many instances, we forget to change beneficiary designations because we always feel we will have time to do that administrative stuff. Probate judges and executors can't override and say, "well I'm sure s/he meant for that asset to go elsewhere." They have to follow the specific written instructions. In that life insurance example, if you pass away and have never updated your beneficiary designation on that policy, you will be making an ex-spouse a beneficiary while your current spouse now does not have the resources they need to continue their lifestyle as your ex is now in receipt of your life insurance proceeds.

Wills are often thought to be deciding document, but not if the assets are titled correctly or have current beneficiary designations marked. Another example where the will is moot is when titling property as **Joint Tenants with Rights of Survivorship (JTWOS)**. If a property is co-owned with JTWROS, even if the will directs disposition to someone else, the co-owner receives the property.

There are some assets that act by virtue of contract law whereby the beneficiary designation supersedes the will and any expressed intent. Life insurance was already provided as an example. Other assets included in this category are qualified retirement plans (e.g.,

IRAs, 401ks/403b) and annuities will pay to the listed beneficiary regardless of wills or other legal documents. In many cases, estate planning attorneys will encourage the beneficiary information to include a primary, e.g., spouse and a secondary or contingent beneficiary, e.g., family trust. Consult with your attorney!

Presumably, after having read these examples, you are thinking, "Does the titling of my assets align with beneficiary designations, wills, and preferences?" It's absolutely critical to take stock of **EVERY** asset; namely, how it's owned, what those ramifications are, and who is named as the beneficiary. Let's avoid having the courts involved in our lives via probate with proper planning.

This entry may have contained some jargon, so here is a brief legend to clarify any confusing terms or strategies regarding account titling.

- **Individually Owned:** solely owned. The Will determines who is beneficiary.
- **Tenants in Common:** separate interests. Each individual owner's Will determines distribution.
- **JTWROS:** co-share. Will is moot. If investment account owned with spouse, spouse will receive at death.
- **Tenants by Entirety:** Spouses only. Both must sign. Again, make sure this is in alignment with overreaching goals.
- **Community Property:** spouses only. Confirm the Will communicates intent.

There are more layers to this essential Protection Strategy, but as it relates to COVID-19, the point is that we never have a better time than the present to get our affairs in order. The people entering the hospital for check-ups on their breathing often never saw their families and advisors after that moment. We do not know what future waves look like nor how quickly the medical community will be able to respond to the next pandemic. You can mitigate these risks by working with your advisor on a quick **Titling and Beneficiary Review**.

We will look at family communication tactics in the third part of our Protection Strategies that covers **Executor and Trustee** selection.

For a comprehensive review of your personal situation, always consult your legal advisor. Neither Cetera Advisors LLC, nor any of its representatives may give legal advice.

EXECUTOR & TRUSTEE SELECTION
ISSUE NUMBER 9 OUT OF 13
SPECIAL PROTECTION STRATEGIES EDITION PART 3 OUT OF 3

This is the final section in our three-part chapter series on Protection Strategies.

Protection Strategies is a catch-all phrase for "getting your ducks in a row" regarding your financial affairs. When we say Protection Strategies, it refers to three "lite estate planning" strategies, **Titling & Beneficiary Designations**, **Planning for Incapacity**, and **Executor and Trustee Selection**. Let's face it, unless you have more than $11 million dollars individually or more than $22 million as a couple, your family doesn't "technically" have an estate planning concern. However, you do have to address the basic challenges of **Legacy Planning** and what to do with your financial assets at the end of life. Titling and Beneficiary Designations address how your assets will transfer and to whom they will transfer upon your passing. Planning for Incapacity addresses who will handle your affairs if you are unable to manage them during life. Executor and Trustee Selection addresses that same issue, only from the lens of handling affairs posthumously.

While it is the third topic we are addressing in this collection of strategies, Executor & Trustee selection is **ESPECIALLY** important. Who is going to be charged with handling your affairs when the time comes? How do we select this individual? What should we be looking for?

Both the Planning for Incapacity and Executor and Trustee Selection really come down to one major decision: Who do you trust the most to carry out your intentions? COVID-19 has taught us that we must always be prepared as we never know when an unexpected illness or accident can happen that prevents us from seeing close family members or our trusted advisors ever again. So why leave this to chance? Why take unnecessary risks? Let's take a look at a couple of things you can do right now to give yourself a better composure and lower the overall risk that your intentions won't be followed.

These are tough choices and you do not have to address them on your own. When engaging this process with our clients, it's recommended to **consider the following items:**

1) **Designate a person or organization you trust and with whom we (and your advisors) are able to continue to work with after death.**
2) **Make sure your executor knows what is asked of them and share your intentions.**
3) **Schedule and hold a meeting with you, your executor, and all of your advisors so that we are all on the same page.**

4) **Schedule and hold a family meeting with your beneficiaries to make sure the family understands your intentions.**

So, what makes a person a great candidate to be your executor? Trustee characteristics often include but are not limited to the following: **trustworthy, legally qualified, willing, maintains financial skills, able to handle assets & liabilities, familiar with estate & objectives, have the time** and **are healthy.** These are basic competencies of someone with the minimum qualifications to be an executor. But beyond these, you must *trust* them. The person you select must be competent, have integrity, and have compassion as being an executor can be time consuming for them and difficult for the heirs and family members.

We provide each of our clients with a **checklist** to help with the Executor selection process:

- ☐ **Communication with designee about their role**
- ☐ **Listing of ALL assets**
- ☐ **Location of said documents are**
- ☐ **Information about your assets**
- ☐ **Copies of legal documents (e.g., wills and trusts)**
- ☐ **Recommendations on communication and interaction with your various advisors**

As wealth strategists, we promise to:

- **Meet with you and your designee.**
- **Provide you with specific confidential communication on this topic.**

- **Take a multi-generational approach, working with ALL family members and designated beneficiaries.**

If you are in private practice and have business partners, we will make sure that you, your family, your partners, and your employees are protected by ensuring you have a documented and funded transition plan. Your partners will be the ones to carry on your business goals and objectives, but who will ensure that your personal intentions and values live on? Your executor or trustee. It's an important choice.

Regarding your financial plan, our promise to you is that we help you effectively pursue your goals during life and make sure that "all of your ducks are in a row" so your intentions become action following your passing. We will help you make sure all of your plans are solidified and documented; all updated and in one place. We will ensure primary executor, successors, and contingencies are all on board with your goals during life and be there to support them following your death.

Death is something that many people are uncomfortable talking about, but in the case of wealth management, the inevitable must be addressed. One of the most crucial decisions a person must make is who to name as Executor under their will or Successor Trustee under a Revocable Living Trust. After that selection is made, you need to make sure that that person is supported with the best information including signed documents, updated beneficiary designations, appropriate account titling, business continuity and transition documents just to name a few.

Have you had this discussion with your lead advisor or wealth strategist? If not, have you considered why not? You are a busy professional seeing patients and meeting with your teams all day. You are busy running your practice and trust that your lead advisor is on top of topics like this. If your advisor hasn't mentioned this and only want to talk about your investible assets and performance, ask yourself "Why?" Why aren't they asking the tough questions about who will be there to make the decisions if you cannot, during life or after your passing. If they are not working in the best interest of you and your family now, what gives you the confidence they will act in your family's best interest when you are unable to direct them.

Death isn't an easy topic to discuss or even think about. As your lead advisor needs to act with integrity, competence, and compassion, there is no greater demonstration of compassion than being willing to have difficult conversations like these now when the financial well-being of your family and your practice depend on the competency and preparedness of your executor.

> *For a comprehensive review of your personal situation, always consult your legal advisor. Neither Cetera Advisors LLC, nor any of its representatives may give legal advice.*

EDUCATION & FAMILY SUPPORT
ISSUE NUMBER 10 OUT OF 13

Taking care of one's family is often one of the most meaningful issues to our clients. It also happens to be one of the most delicate issues. Often overlooked by clients and advisors alike is the difficult subject of the next phase of planning; namely, two items. What are your wishes as aging and potential incapacity occurs, as well as how would you like your family to receive your legacy? Although difficult to discuss in some cases, having all these factors to your plan spelled out with clear understandable wishes and expectations, actually results in a significantly improved family dynamic.

Let's begin with the drivers of family support/gifting. Typically, there are **four primary considerations**:

1) **Educational Planning:** There are myriad options, however the commonly known strategies include: 529 plans, Coverdale Education Funds, prepaid tuition programs, and Uniform Gift/Trust to Minor (UGMA/UTMA). It's important, as with all vehicles, to discuss with your wealth strategist the appropriate vehicles for your goals.

2) **Reduction of Estate Taxes:** For some folks, they are able to accomplish two objectives at once. Help support their family while *also* significantly reducing estate taxes. Options include cash donations during life, gifting shares of appreciable stock, land within an FLP or LLC, utilizing various gifting strategies whereby the value of assets are compressed or perhaps shares with restrictions resulting in discounted pricing, are a few of many to consider.

3) **Passing on Family Values:** Often clients feel a personal responsibility to make sure their values are passed on and extended to future generations. Through the wealth transfer process and by working with an attorney, clients are able to set particular parameters and expectations to future generations with respect to philanthropy, stewardship, and education.

4) **Eldercare:** There are four integrated issues to consider when planning for eldercare objectives. First, incapacity. No decision-making ability. Powers of attorney, rights, revocable trusts, trustee, and successors are all part of this discussion. The goal is to avoid going to court. Second, health care considerations. HIPAA and disclosures are especially important when children are at college. Parents and children must have this worked out in advance. Third, directives. Bottom line, denote how care will be administered. Fourth, Medicare/LTC. A.B.C.D. What covers what and how and how much? Medi-gap potentially to bridge from A to D? Do

we consider long-term care insurance to potentially offer in-home care?

In many cases, people are uncomfortable or unfamiliar with how to engage this process. Here are a number of **potential questions/topics** to consider in your household (all family members included):

1) **What are your plans? What are you going to do? Where/how will you spend time?**
2) **Have you involved your children in the decision-making?**
3) **What are your plans for your children? Parents?**
4) **Are there other family members to consider?**
5) **Are you prepared for 24/7 care with Alzheimer's or other debilitations?**
6) **What would an ideal world look like for you with respect to education funding, family values, incapacity, and estate taxes?**

Our experience is the difficulty lies in engaging the initial dialogues. However, with a reasonable framework and guidance from advisors, before you know it all members of the family are on the same page and feeling secure in the plans laid out.

CHARITABLE & PHILANTHROPIC GIVING
ISSUE NUMBER 11 OUT OF 13

As one can imagine, charitable giving is of great important to many people for a variety of reasons. Some folks are focused on tax efficiency and others are concerned with control issues. In some cases, people want to leave a legacy and have solidly altruistic objectives in mind. More recently, families with multiple generations are seeking to be more inclusive within the family about charitable causes and how the family makes donations in general. Whatever the reasons, diligent planning is critical to optimize outcomes. These outcomes can often be summarized in one sentence:

Maximize clients' usable dollars while minimizing the tax burden.

One of the first things to consider regarding planned giving is the difference between **Charitably Inclined** and **Philanthropically Motivated**. The difference lies in the focus and motivations. Being charitably inclined results in support to many different causes whereas philanthropically motivated involves a narrow focus, for example, a particular university, church or cause. In either case, it's important to recognize the motivations present while also incorporating potential family dynamics and other financial goals. Included with this discussion is clearly articulating the **three greatest risks** when considering charitable giving:

1) **Not understanding all the alternatives:** Often folks think someone else has it covered. It's important to be proficient with current tax law, have expertise in trusts/family foundations (FF), as well as comfort with Donor Advised Fund (DAF). There are ways you can donate your capital or appreciating stock and make a difference, but there are other options as well; including using your family's intellectual and social influence to raise awareness.

2) **Experiencing a loss of influence/control:** Outright gifts result in NO control. Consider FF & DAF to maintain influence.

3) **Paying too much in taxes:** Pretty straightforward, thematically, however there are enumerable strategies to consider based on objectives. Taxes should never surprise you. Your advisor should be able to explain how charitable gifts can be structured for both tax efficiency and maximum control.

Now that the three greatest risks have been covered, let's move to the **three primary modalities** for Planned Giving: **Direct Transfers, Indirect Transfers** and **Split Interest Transfers**. For purposes of this entry, the topics will be kept VERY lean. There is an incredible amount of detail which needs to be reviewed with your advisors on a collaborative basis.

1) **Direct Transfers:** Donor to recipient. Cash or check. Likely not the most effective from a tax perspective or when considering control. Thus, perhaps evaluating modality #2 is sensible.

2) **Indirect Transfers:** Donor Advised Funds. Pooled Fund. Family Foundation. Maintain control and potentially significant tax reduction. What if the organization or institution to which your philanthropic motivations changed values? With Direct Transfers there is no recourse. With Indirect Transfers, you simply change the direction of the donations.

3) **Split Transfers:** Split interest gifts whereby the value is split between the charity and another entity, beneficiary, etc. There are THREE types of Split Transfers. Again, due to space, the suggestion is to consult your advisors for greater detail. The first option is a **Charitable Remainder Trust (CRT)** with two sub-categories including **Charitable Remainder Annuity Trust (CRAT)** and **Charitable Remainder Unit Trust (CRUT)**. In summary, a certain amount is donated into the CRT. The beneficiary or donor receives payments from the trust until the trust terminates whereupon the proceeds transfer to the philanthropic organization. Taxes are reduced significantly if structured properly. The second option is a **Pooled Income Fund** which works for benefit of

universities. Much like the CRT strategy, the donor, donor's spouse, or beneficiary receive an income stream on a pro rata basis with residual assets transferring to the university upon termination. The final option is a **Charitable Lead Trust (CLT)**. The CLT works in the inverse to the CRT, whereby the charity receives an income stream for a set period of time and the remaining balance transfers to a designated beneficiary. CLTs have an entirely different tax element associated with them and should be coordinated with experts.

All of this said, there are ways that you can be charitable, philanthropic, and bring your second and/or third generation into the financial decisions of your family. Consider that the benefits of Charitable and Philanthropic Giving outlined above all center around the use of financial capital. Financial capital is one of **four common types** of capital that individuals and families can use to bring about change in their community or on a wider stage. Besides **financial capital**, there is **intellectual capital, social capital**, and **human capital**.

You may find yourself in a situation where you want to give to certain causes or organizations more than you can or that is strategically financially sound. In these cases, you can leverage these other types of capital to achieve results. Consider that you may have a goal to donate $1 million dollars to fight heart disease due to the passing of a loved one caused by that disease. Yet financially, you may only be able to donate $300,000 and still achieve your other financial goals. In this example, you might consider hosting a fundraiser or other type of event to raise awareness. Here you are using your intellectual capital and social capital, or your personal or family's influence, to draw more affluent people to the cause or event. This can have the same effect as you donating $1 million dollars. In fact, if your family were to harness all of it's human, intellectual, and social capital for a few years in a row hosting an event or fundraiser, you may be able to exceed your goal and create broader awareness.

You should feel comfortable discussing these types of charitable and philanthropic goals with your advisor. Your advisor can likely speak with your entire family about the causes that are important to them and then cover the ways that your financial, human, intellectual, and social capital can be leveraged to bring about their social goals. Giving is an important financial strategy. You can benefit import causes, reap incredible tax benefits, and potentially get closer with your 2nd and 3rd generations in the family by leveraging all of your family's capital, not just your financial capital to achieve your charitable or philanthropic goals.

Charitable Remainder Trust: Such trusts are used to develop a vehicle for donations to a favorite charity, which also allows for the reduction of income taxes through a charitable deduction and favorable tax treatment at the date of the gift by non-recognition of built-in capital gains.

The use of trusts involves a complex web of tax rules and regulations. You should consider the counsel of an experienced estate planning professional before implementing such strategies.

For a comprehensive review of your personal situation, always consult your legal advisor. Neither Cetera Advisors LLC, nor any of its representatives may give legal advice.

A CLEAN BILL OF WEALTH

DISTRIBUTION OF ESTATE
ISSUE NUMBER 12 OUT OF 13

When you consider the traditional financial path the majority of Americans take towards wealth creation, there are typically four phases: **Accumulation, Transition, Decumulation,** and **Transfer.** Transfer is referring to the transfer of financial assets to spouses, children, partners, or charitable causes through the **Distribution of Estate**. The Distribution of Estate has incredible meaning to folks having built their wealth, their business, their imprint on society and on life. You've spent your entire life developing your wealth, providing lessons to your heirs and now it's time to effectively and specifically transfer that which you've worked so diligently to build.

The term "Estate" can be misleading as there are different uses of the word. At its core, it can be used to describe things like money and property that are accumulated by a person during their life, and which needs to be disposed or distributed at their death. Unless there are wills or trusts guiding the distribution, the person's remaining estate may have to go through a probate court. Estate can also be used to just think about a person's real estate holding.

In truth, only a very few Americans have Estate Planning tax issues and challenges. As the Estate Tax is handled by Congress, it is important to recognize that thresholds and exemptions on various taxes, including the Estate Tax, will change from time to time. As of today, unless a family has a combined net-worth of more than $22 million dollars, they don't yet have an Estate Tax situation. As the Estate Tax is impacting fewer families, the spotlight is shifting to the type of legacy they will leave behind rather than focusing on the tax considerations only. The same tools, legal, and financial instruments which are used to transfer financial assets can also be used to transfer family values as well.

So, when we combine the financial aspects and the value aspect, there are **four common** Estate & Legacy planning goals shared by many of our clients. They are: **Maximize Wealth Transfer, Minimize the Transfer Tax, Optimizing Control or Influence**, and finally **Transferring Family Values.** Let's break down each one separately:

1) **Maximize Wealth Transfer:** Said plainly, we help families align their assets with their dispositive documents so they are consistent with their wishes, regulations, and taxes. It is important to ensure all of your assets are titled appropriately, that you have beneficiaries clearly updated, and that documents like your wills and trusts are updated, aligned, and readily accessible.

2) **Minimize the Transfer Tax:** There is a certain amount of money which transfers without paying a transfer tax. There is

an unlimited transfer to spouses. There are three ways to fulfill personal and tax objectives: **Testamentary Exemption Amount, Marital Trust**, and **Unlimited Charitable Deduction**. Other issues to consider when minimizing the transfer tax include tax efficiency, estate liquidity, a QTIP, and a QDOT (for non-US citizen spouse). Each of these options requires diligence and expert counsel to know which to implement. As a business owner, know that we pay extra attention to the structure of your practice to ensure that your business transitions with minimal tax implications as well.

3) **Optimizing Control or Influence:** There are a number of considerations here that should be reviewed. If you have a family member with special needs, we can help you to consider a special needs trust. You may have special circumstances where beneficiaries engage in poor behaviors. We can help you consider different types of incentive-based trusts which provides beneficiaries with qualifiers, e.g., drug screening, jobs based, education based, etc. to receive benefits. The more we know about your family dynamics, the better we can recommend the right solutions for those family dynamics.

4) **Transferring Family Values:** There are ways to use trusts to help you instill your family values into future generations; or to reinforce them. There are ways to tie distributions to heirs' involvement with charities/philanthropic efforts, both with

respect to participation and financial distributions if giving is important to you. There are also other requirements that can be placed on education in order to receive distributions.

The bottom line is that there are strategies that can be used to help you transfer your values to future generations, not just your financial assets. This is important as you do not want to make your last days someone else's first day that they never have to work or give again. We work to understand where motivations lie and then plan where and to whom the legacy is directed in a manner congruent with the values of the donor.

There are many questions to consider when developing your transfer plan. Here is a list of some of those to help you begin the process:

1) **Are you certain that your distribution plan at death provides for the maximum amount of your wealth to pass free of taxes to your beneficiaries & heirs?**
2) **Do you wish to leave all assets outright to heirs OR does the concept of leaving wealth in a donor-advised fund to be used and distribute toward your wishes make sense? How prepared will your children be for inheritance by the time they receive a distribution under your plan?**
3) **What types of family conversations have you had regarding your estate plan?**
4) **How have you coordinated the titling of assets to facilitate your plan?**
5) **What is most important to you? Does your plan reward**

hard work?

6) Since the change in circumstance occurs, are you willing to let your spouse/children make decisions after you are gone?

In our firm, we use INHERIT as a means by which to walk clients through the plan development process.

I - Integrated choices: Who. What. How much. How to distribute.

N - Non-tax Reasons: Special needs. Special assets. Business owners and succession.

H - Heirs: Spouse. Re-marriage issues. Children. Grandchildren. Involvement. Charity.

E - Experienced Professional Advice: Coordinated advisory team - management & distribution.

R - Relating Your Plan: Plan communicated? How is it managed? Does family understand?

I - Implementation: Who will implement? Family? Corporation? Combination?

T - Tax Elimination/Minimization: Transfer tax is voluntary. How much to pay?

The use of the acronym, INHERIT, helps to consider choices a high-net-worth individual must address. There is no "one-size-fits-all" estate plan that works for every family and every business owner. There are several considerations, and it often takes several meetings to refine your plan. Not all of these choices are easy or pleasant to discuss, but failure to address these items ensures you have no input and that the courts will have a greater say in how and when your assets are distributed. We consider the choices made, your current situation and steps already taken. Our approach is one of caution and great detail in order to provide you with the peace of mind that your financial assets and values will transfer to your family and designated institutions in the way that you choose.

TAX PLANNING
ISSUE NUMBER 13 OUT OF 13

Well, we made it to Wealth Management Issue #13: **Tax Planning**. You might be saying, "I already have a CPA for taxes for the business and family, what's the connection to my investments?" Or, "I don't think we qualify for the estate tax, so we are all set." Our perspective is that we believe tax planning underpins each of the other issues that we have discussed in this book. As a financial planning firm, we ask questions to understand your perspectives on tax and provide planning strategies on how to achieve your goals in the most tax-efficient manner possible. While we do not give direct tax advice, we are "tax-aware" of the implications that one set of financial decisions will have on your current and future financial picture.

Tax Planning isn't just about deductions, it includes looking at how your retirement plans are structured. You might have previous 401(k) plans from a previous hospital employer and have the current plan you offer to your employees. The decision to roll over and how to do it has significant tax implications that require planning.

Depending on your goals, it may be more efficient to use insurance to transfer wealth to future generations and donate portions of your portfolio to maximize any charitable deductions. Tax is a part of your entire financial picture.

Coordination between your CPA and lead advisory or financial planning firm is key. Based on the investment performance and goals, it's critical to coordinate with your other advisors like your CPA.

We work together with your other advisors to make the best possible recommendations within your financial plan. Here are the **nine key Tax Planning Strategies** that we will explore.

1) **Tax-Efficient Investing:** It's what you keep, not what you make.

2) **Adjusted Tax Withholdings:** No sense in providing the IRS with a tax-free loan.

3) **Tax Loss Harvesting:** Utilize these losses to offset gains in the future.

4) **$3,000 Capital Loss Opportunity:** Against marginal rates = more savings.

5) **Charitable Contributions:** Direct transfer? Appreciated property/stock? Donor-Advised Funds for causes.

6) **Reinvested Dividends:** If declared it's taxed - be mindful.

7) **Qualified & Non-Qualified Retirement Plans:** Lower taxes today and in the future with balance.

8) **Accelerated State & Local Taxes:** Evaluate with CPA to determine effectiveness.

9) **Transitioning Current Assets:** Discuss your vision for the

eventual sale of a business. Decisions now impact options and outcomes in the future.

After reviewing these strategies with you and your CPA, your plan will likely be set to pursue your goals effectively in the most tax-efficient way possible. The greatest risk is paying too much in taxes by not being aware of or utilizing appropriate means for deductions, exclusions, credits, and donations. As wealth strategists, our role is to look at separate aspects of your financial life making certain these work together for the best outcomes.

How often are you meeting with your financial planner and your CPA together? If you have outside investments, are those managers included in the coordination? If these meetings aren't happening, why not? We are experienced at bringing these types of disparate advisors together to align your plan with the smartest tax strategies possible.

For a comprehensive review of your personal situation, always consult with a tax or legal advisor. Neither Cetera Advisors LLC nor any of its representatives may give legal or tax advice.

CONCLUSION

Well, we've come to the end of this journey together.

Thirteen Wealth Management Issues.

Comprehensive/Holistic Wealth Management.

An **integration** and **confluence** of myriad wealth planning topics designed to lead you to success, achieving your financial goals.

Some of the topics here may not apply to your particular situation. However, know that a **Certified Wealth Strategist** is reviewing all of these issues as part of their defined and systematic process to ensure your plan and your outcomes are congruent with your objectives and timelines.

Hopefully you've learned a few things. Perhaps some of the information here caused some degree of distress. That's good. Identifying the gaps and moving closer to solutions is the goal. Years ago, another advisor we heard speak would routinely say this: What happens if you ignore cancer?

It gets bigger, badder, and worse.

He would then pivot to, "How quickly would you want to know you had cancer?" Of course, the response was always "As soon as possible!"

Certainly, one of the goals in writing this manual is to educate. However, another goal is to prompt thought...even concern. Perhaps some of the questions coming to mind include:

- **Am I doing everything I can do to mitigate the impact of taxation?**
- **Is my legal planning done correctly?**
- **When was the last time I reviewed beneficiary information?**
- **Have I conducted a thorough risk management analysis?**
- **Is my investment portfolio properly diversified and congruent with my risk profile?**

Surely there are other questions, too. Know that for these and any other questions or concerns that arise, you have a resource. We are here to guide you through your situation, comprehensively making certain to cover and discuss all applicable Wealth Management Issues.

Time to take action. Time to provide certainty. Time to cover all the bases.

A CLEAN BILL OF WEALTH

ABOUT THE AUTHORS

ANTHONY C. WILLIAMS
CWS, CHFC, MRFC, CLU
INVESTMENT ADVISOR
REPRESENTATIVE

Mr. Williams is a Certified Wealth Strategist (CWS), Chartered Financial Consultant (ChFC), Master Registered Financial Consultant (MRFC), and Chartered Life Underwriter (CLU). For over 20 years, he has worked with specialty doctors providing guidance with designing, implementing, monitoring, and evaluating holistic wealth management services at all phases of career and all stages of life. This experience led to the emergence of his newest brand, the Orthopaedist Advisory Group, which provides Orthopaedic Surgeons and their families strategies to accumulate wealth and help to lessen overall risk for increased financial confidence. His work in finance also sees him stepping away from the office onto a larger stage, and you will frequently find him appearing across the country as a featured keynote speaker on issues pertinent to Orthopaedic Surgeons at physician groups, annual Orthopaedic Trauma and California Orthopaedic Associations meetings, and teaching hospitals. He is also a frequent speaker at the American Academy of Orthopaedic Surgeons annual meeting. Anthony's services encompass a broad range of solutions to these issues including, but not limited to, asset protection management, student-debt payoff strategies, retirement funding, tax planning, and more.

ABOUT THE AUTHORS

CHRIS NEKVINDA, PHD

Dr. Nekvinda is a highly accomplished and talented learning and organizational development leader with a proven record of success in training/development, instructional design, e-learning, adult learning, organizational development, leadership training, change management, curriculum development, orientation programs, performance consulting, sales development, and technical writing. He develops and implements strategic linkage between business objectives, leadership, and employees in multi-faceted environments, emphasizing design, delivery, and evaluation of systems. Many of his specialties include wealth management, private banking, premier banking, insurance, investment management, systems thinking, research, testing and evaluation, instructional design, performance-centered design, game theory, and performance support. Dr. Nekvinda currently serves as Senior Vice President and Director of Global Learning Operations at Cannon Financial Institute. He has responsibility for consulting, instructional design, program materials, and content creation. In addition, he leads all organizational change management projects for Cannon.

www.ingramcontent.com/pod-product-compliance
Lightning Source LLC
Chambersburg PA
CBHW040227220526
45473CB00001B/153